lithgow palooza reade

It Stinks to be Extinct!

By Susan Blackaby

School Specialty Publishing

Text Copyright © 2007 School Specialty Publishing. Manatee Character © 2003 by John Lithgow. Manatee Illustration © 2003 by Ard Hoyt.

Library of Congress Cataloging-in-Publication Data is on file with the publisher.

Send all inquiries to:
School Specialty Publishing
8720 Orion Place
Columbus, OH 43240-2111

ISBN 0-7696-4254-3

1 2 3 4 5 6 7 8 9 10 PHXBK 12 11 10 09 08 07 06

Table of Contents

Manatee

Manatees are also called *sea cows*.
These **marine** mammals spend their days
eating plants in shallow water along the coast.
They swim between salt and freshwater
marshes, bays, and estuaries.
For many years, it has been against the law in the
United States to harm or hunt marine mammals.
However, these laws cannot save manatees
from **extinction**.
People have taken over **habitats** where
manatees feed.
People in boats run over manatees by accident.
The manatees cannot swim fast enough to get
out of the way.
Today, there may be only 2,500 manatees left in
the wild.

Manatee Mentions
Speedboats kill more than 100 manatees a year.

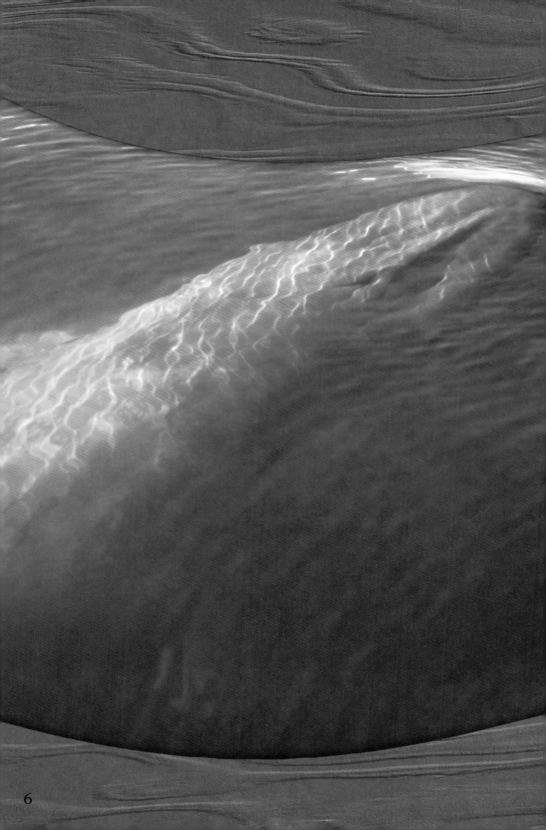

Blue Whale

Blue whales are marine mammals that live
in all the oceans on the earth.
In the winter, blue whales **migrate** to warm waters
near the equator.
They spend spring and summer
in the **polar** regions.
For many years, people hunted whales for their oil.
People used the whale oil to make soaps, candles,
and lamp oil.
Their population began to **decrease**.
They almost became extinct.
Then, countries around the world agreed to stop
hunting them.
Today, the number of blue whales is
slowly increasing.

Manatee Mentions
The blue whale is the largest creature that has ever
lived on the earth. It is even bigger than the dinosaurs!

Sea Turtle

Sea turtles live in warm coastal waters.
Female sea turtles leave the water
to lay eggs in the sand.
Many animals hunt and eat turtle eggs.
Human beings also cause problems for sea turtles.
Every year, fishing nets trap more than
10,000 sea turtles.
Bright lights from homes, stores, and restaurants
scare nesting sea turtles.
The bright lights confuse baby sea turtles trying
to get to the water after they are born.
Sea turtles also get sick and die from eating trash
that looks like food.
Unless people change their habits,
sea turtles will soon disappear from the earth.

Manatee Mentions

The leatherback sea turtle has lived on the earth for 100 million years. But, it may become extinct before the year 2020.

Snake River Salmon

Hundreds of years ago, millions of salmon
filled the rivers of the western United States.
People and animals came to depend
on the salmon for food.
As the western United States grew, people built
dams on the rivers.
The dams create waterways and supply power.
But the dams also block adult salmon
from swimming upstream to lay their eggs.
The dams block baby salmon as they migrate
downriver to the sea.
If salmon are to survive there, the rivers need
to flow freely again.

Manatee Mentions

Salmon return to the streams where they were born to
lay eggs. Some salmon travel nearly 1,000 miles from the
ocean to the mountain streams of Idaho and Washington.

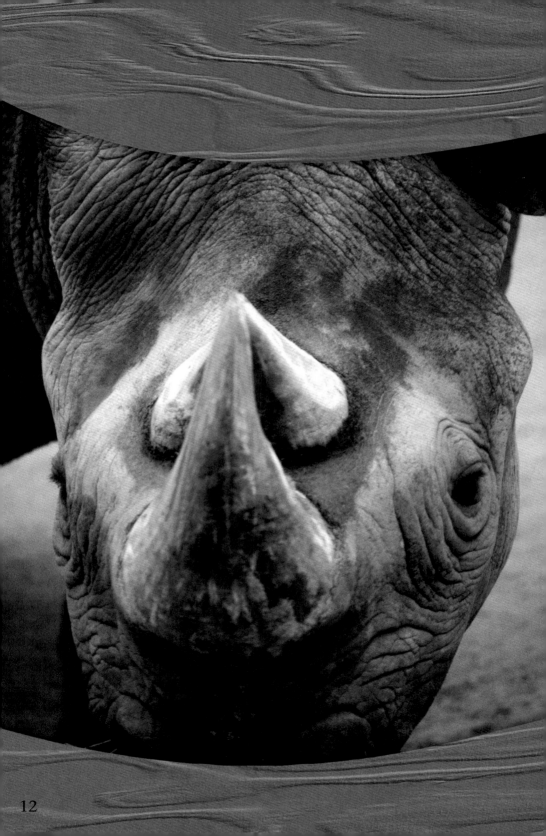

Black Rhinoceros

The word *rhinoceros* is Greek for "horn-nosed."
Rhinos use their horns for protection.
They also use their horns to dig for food.
Black rhinos once lived in many parts of Africa.
Little by little, people started moving into rhino
habitats and taking over the land.
Many rhinos were killed because they were
a threat to people's safety.
People hunted black rhinos for their meat
and their skin.
People still use rhino horns to make knife handles.
And they grind up the horns to make medicine.
The black rhino will not survive unless
this hunting stops.

Manatee Mentions

Most black rhinos have two horns. One of these horns is
almost 20 inches long, about the length of your arm!

King Cobra

The king cobra is the biggest poisonous snake
on the earth.
It can grow up to 18 feet long—
about as long as two cars!
When it is mad or excited, the king cobra
flares out its neck like a hood.
The poison from its bite can kill an elephant.
King cobras live near water in the rainforests,
woods, swamps, and grasslands of Asia.
People are the adult king cobra's only **predator**.
People kill cobras because they are afraid of them.
They trap the cobras to sell them.
They turn cobra habitats into farmland.

Manatee Mentions

Right now, king cobras are not **endangered**. They are
threatened in parts of India. This means they are
likely to become endangered in the future if people do
not stop killing them.

Coral Reef

Corals are tiny sea animals that live in groups.
As they die, their shells join together
to make a base where more corals can grow.
Layers of coral build up over years and years
to make a reef.
A coral reef is a habitat for many other
sea creatures.
Corals need shallow salt water that is clean
and warm.
Rising sea levels and global warming threaten
coral reefs.
So does **pollution** from oil spills, trash,
and wastewater.

Manatee Mentions
Acid from old batteries that are dumped into the
ocean eats away at coral reefs.

Mountain Gorilla

Mountain gorillas look powerful,
but they are very gentle.
They travel in small groups to find food.
A full-grown male, called a *silverback*,
acts as the group's leader.
He protects his group from danger.
These gorillas live high in the mountains
of East Africa.
But people have destroyed most of their
forest habitat.
People cut down trees to build homes
and create farmland.
Today, there are only two small areas
where these gorillas can be found.

Manatee Mentions

There may be fewer than 600 mountain gorillas left in the wild.

Giant Panda

Giant pandas are known
for their black and white markings.
They live in the bamboo forests of China.
The pandas are endangered
because they are running out of food.
Pandas eat bamboo.
This bamboo grows in only a few places.
When pandas run out of food,
they must travel to find more.
Sometimes, the new bamboo is too far away.
Sometimes, people build roads and towns
that block the way to the new bamboo.
Today, only about 1,000 pandas are left
in the wild.

Manatee Mentions

The giant panda is the symbol of the WWF (formerly
known as the World Wildlife Fund). The WWF has been
working to save endangered animals since the 1960s.

Grizzly Bear

Grizzly bears, also called *brown bears*,
are named for their shaggy fur.
The bears once roamed the United States
from the Great Plains to the West Coast.
Little by little, people moved west
and took over the bears' habitat.
People hunted grizzlies for their fur and meat.
They also killed grizzlies to keep their cattle safe
from bear attacks.
Today, 30,000 grizzly bears live in the wilderness
of Alaska.
However, there are only about 1,000 grizzlies left
in the lower 48 states.

Manatee Mentions

Biologists use satellite technology to track bears as
they move from place to place.

Tiger

The tiger is the largest member of the cat family.
It once lived throughout Asia.
In the last 100 years, three tiger **species**
have become extinct.
Five species are endangered.
There may be fewer than 7,000 tigers left in the wild.
Tigers hunt large and small mammals.
Their light fur and dark stripes help them hide
while they are hunting.
But people have cleared land in the tigers' habitat.
When land is cleared, the tigers have nowhere
to hide.
They go hungry because they cannot sneak up on
their **prey**.

Manatee Mentions

The Big Cat Rescue Group is located in Tampa, Florida.
This group provides homes for mistreated and
abandoned wild cats.

Drill Monkey

A drill monkey is a large **primate**.
It looks like a baboon and travels in large
family groups of 20 or more monkeys.
For thousands of years, these monkeys lived quietly
in far-off places in Africa.
Then, hunters started hunting drill monkeys
for their meat.
The meat sold for a high price at the market.
Today, people have set aside land to protect
and study drill monkeys in their habitat.
Drill monkeys do not thrive in zoos.
So, it is important to protect drill monkeys
in the wild.

Manatee Mentions

Drill monkeys are Africa's most endangered primates.
They are in serious need of protection.

Bald Eagle

The bald eagle is named for its white head.
It appears to be hairless from a distance.
The bald eagle is a familiar symbol
in the United States.
But 40 years ago, it would have been rare to see one.
At that time, people used the chemical DDT
to control pests.
DDT killed bugs that carried illnesses and ate crops.
But it also harmed the eggshells of baby birds.
The eggs cracked before the baby birds could hatch.
As a result, the number of bald eagles decreased.
DDT was banned in 1972.
Since then, the number of bald eagles has grown.
The bald eagle is still listed as a threatened species
in every state except Alaska.

Manatee Mentions

Bald eagles flock to the northwest coast of the United
States. The salmon there are a main food source for the
bald eagle.

Vocabulary

decrease–to become less in number. *Pollution in the ocean water causes the number of sea turtles to decrease.*

endangered–in danger of becoming extinct. *The king cobra is not yet endangered.*

habitat–a place where an animal or a plant naturally grows and lives. *People have taken over the tigers' habitat.*

extinction–no longer existing. *The extinction of the dinosaurs happened millions of years ago.*

marine–having to do with the sea. *The manatee is an endangered marine mammal.*

migrate–to move from one place to another. *Salmon migrate from streams to the sea.*

polar–having to do with the North Pole or the South Pole. *The ocean water in the polar regions is very cold.*

pollution–the state of being dirty or impure. *Oil spills cause water pollution.*

predator–an animal that hunts and eats other animals for food. *The sea turtle's eggs were eaten by a predator.*

prey–an animal that is hunted by another animal for food. *The eagle swoops down to grab its prey out of the water.*

primate–a mammal of the order *Primates*, that includes monkeys, apes, and human beings, with a large brain and flexible hands. *The drill monkey is an endangered primate.*

species–a group of living things that have similar traits. *Snake River Salmon are a species of fish.*

threatened–likely to become endangered. *The king cobra is threatened in parts of India.*

Think About It!

1. How do boating laws help protect manatees?

2. How does human activity harm sea turtles?

3. What do corals need in order to survive?

4. How does the loss of its habitat hurt tigers?

5. What might happen to bald eagles if salmon become extinct?

The Story and You!

1. Which animal from the book would you like to learn more about? Why?

2. How could you plan a community where animals and people live side by side?

3. Brainstorm some ways that you could help threatened and endangered animals.

4. Which animal would you choose to be the symbol for saving wildlife? Explain your choice.

5. Do you think it is important to keep animals from becoming extinct? Why or why not?

Other *Lithgow Palooza*™ Readers your child can enjoy:

Level Two	Level Three	Level Four
Tweet, Oompa, Bumpety-Boom!	Music Around the World	Sing, Strum, and Beat the Drum!
Moo-Moo Went the Tuba	Sounds of Celebration!	Rock, Rag, and Swing
A Crash, a Roar, and So Much More!	A Den, a Tree, a Nest Is Best	Pockets That Hop
Slither, Slide, Hop, and Run	The Amazing, Incredible You!	Zippety Zoo
Salty, Sandy, Soggy Homes	Drop, Drip, an Underwater Trip	Who's in Your Class?
Splishy, Splashy Mammals	Sea Cows Don't Moo!	It Stinks to Be Extinct!

lithgow palooza readers

Animals need our respect and attention, too! Take a look at the different endangered animals at risk of becoming extinct and learn what is currently being done to save them. John Lithgow is dedicated to introducing developing readers to the wonderful worlds of arts and literacy. Turn the page and join his Manatee character on a fascinating, fun reading adventure!

Guided Reading Level: M
Interest Level: Grades K–4

EMERGING READER Grades K–1

EMERGING 2 READER

- repetitive language
- familiar and unfamiliar vocabulary
- longer sentences

CONFIDENT READER Grades 1–2

CONFIDENT 3 READER

- minimal repetition
- challenging vocabulary; unfamiliar words
- varied, complex sentences

INDEPENDENT READER Grades 2–3

INDEPENDENT 4 READER

- no repetition
- more complex vocabulary
- challenging sentence structure

U.S. $3.95
Can. $5.45
ISBN 0-7696-4254-3

ALIGNED TO STATE & NATIONAL STANDARDS

School Specialty Publishing

Visit our Web site at:
www.SchoolSpecialtyPublishing.com

EAN
ISBN 0-7696-4254-3

9 780769 642543
50395

UPC

0 87577 91954 6
04254